JOSEPH ST

A Life From Beginning to End

Copyright © 2016 by Hourly History Limited

All rights reserved.

Table of Contents

A Change of Weather
The Real Revolution Begins
From Exile to Supreme Leader
A Brave New Word
Stalin's Gambit
Stalin Makes a Comeback
Defending the Capitol
Going West

Introduction

When most Americans think of the "Man of Steel," images of the DC Comics' iconic Superman no doubt come to mind, the safe and salient American hero who appeared in the pulp fiction pages of American comic books beginning in 1938. However, there was another Man of Steel that had emerged over a decade prior to this superhero's debut - and this man of steel was forged under completely different circumstances.

Instead of crash landing on Earth from planet Krypton, Stalin's man of steel was forged in the physical fires of the gulag and the emotional fires of childhood abandonment. He was a man that was often mistreated in life, and as a consequence, he hardened. Every aspect of his personality became as hard as iron, and it was in recognition and dedication to this feat that the man who was born Iosif Dzhugashvili announced to the world that he would be forevermore known as "Stalin," the "Man of Steel."

The man who then took on this mantle of emotional disconnection and dehumanization would spend the rest of his life working to inflict his cold vision on the rest of the world. However, despite his wish to be as solid as steel, Stalin would become an increasingly erratic figure. He often contradicted himself; while he had an inborn desire to involve others in the political process, at the same time he was an iron-fisted despot in constant fear of someone else moving against his will.

In his heart he was a true believer in Marxist ideology and wished to see the communist system, with its equal delegation of powers, take off. Yet his inflexibility and refusal to relinquish his dictatorial powers meant his desire for a Marxist paradise would never get off the runway.

Stalin, a lifelong revolutionary, wished to encourage his love of activism in the common people of the Soviet Union, but the instant the very people he encouraged became "too politically active" he had them thrown in prison. Stalin presents himself as a kind of Russian matryoshka doll—the kind that has layer upon layer of different faces and dress underneath— and it's the complex duplicity of Stalin's multiple layers has left us digging deeper and deeper into his strange personality. Even doing so has left researchers feeling as if they have just barely scratched the surface.

Chapter One

A Change of Weather

"Catch a man a fish, and you can sell it to him. Teach a man to fish, and you ruin a wonderful business opportunity."

—Karl Marx

Stalin was born on December 18th, 1878, in a frontier town on the edge of what then comprised the Russian Empire of Tsar Alexander II. The land of his birth was a recent acquisition in what is known today as Georgia. Despite a common Russian animus at the time for anything Georgian, when Stalin would eventually come to power, he fully embraced his Georgian heritage.

However, for the young man born with the Georgian name of Iosif Dzhugashvili – a name that most Russians had trouble even pronouncing - the likelihood that the child of this backwater region would rise up to any sort of prominence at all would have seemed incredibly unlikely. He was the son of a cobbler and a housemaid who barely made enough money to survive.

When the family's financial situation later moved from bad to worse, his father would turn increasingly to alcohol and the abuse of his family—especially the young Iosif—in order to release the feelings of desperation and rage that he felt. Iosif's mother became increasingly concerned for her son, and in the midst of their struggle came to the conclusion that the only way for him to escape the turmoil was to send him off to seminary school. This is the impetus that brought Stalin to the town of Tiflis—to one of Georgia's local Greek Orthodox monasteries—to become a priest.

Iosif's new peaceful life as a priest got off to a rough start. In 1899 he was expelled from the school after getting into a fight with a local chief of police. Joseph Stalin himself would later claim that he was expelled for disseminating Marxist propaganda. To date, however, it remains unclear whether Stalin's admission was propaganda in itself because there is no other indication besides Stalin's own remarks that Marxism had anything to do with his dismissal.

This may have been one of many of Stalin's attempts at revisionist history when it came to his own personal narrative. Regardless of the actual cause, Stalin's dismissal would be a turning point for the man who would one day become Joseph Stalin, the Man of Steel. Not wishing to return to his parents' broken home, despite his dismissal Joseph decided to stay in Tiflis. It was here at around 21 years of age that he found work at the Tiflis Meteorological Observatory.

This was not due to any known interest in meteorology but rather an act of necessity, and apparently, the only job that Stalin could find. At the dawn of the 20th century the entire Russian Empire was economically depressed, but none more so than frontier regions like Stalin's Georgia. Most of the young men of

Tiflis were unemployed and reduced to panhandling; any number of these destitute Georgians would have jumped at the chance of steady work at the observatory.

Stalin, already knowing the value of being connected, had help landing this job. A good friend of his from his hometown already held a position at the facility, and with just a few good words managed to get Stalin not only a job but a place to stay. He was given a small room to sleep in when he wasn't working, right underneath the observatory.

It was the first solid room and board Stalin had since his expulsion from seminary school. For all of this, it was only required of Stalin to man the post for 3 days a week, making notes of the current temperature and barometer readings. With his basic survival ensured, Stalin now found himself with enough extra time on his hands to delve into the political intrigue of his day.

For Georgia, this meant a heady dose of nationalist desire to break away from Russia and a populist spirit of self-determination. It was here that Stalin became involved with some of the local worker's unions and began to organize strikes on their behalf; with his own employment secure, he sought to influence the employment of others. These efforts would come to a head when he worked to mobilize workers at a local railroad to strike against their employer.

With local industrialists growing increasingly enraged by his disruptive activities, the local police stormed into the Tiflis Observatory and took Stalin into custody. Although organizing peaceful demonstrations was not technically against the law, the police sought to send a clear message to Stalin. Whatever they told him during his detention, however, fell on deaf ears, and Stalin was only emboldened to work even harder to spark a revolution.

With several successful strikes and protests under his belt, Stalin made quite a name for himself as a political activist. As his successes in the field increased he would soon have to give up his day job completely in favor of being a full-time revolutionary agent. After a series of attention-getting demonstrations, Stalin and his cohorts began planning a massive worker's march on Tiflis.

The Tsar's secret police got word of this, however, and decided to round up the movement's leaders to prevent the protest from breaking out. Already knowing where Stalin worked, several police immediately surrounded the observatory, hoping to catch him upon his return. It would prove a bit too obvious, however, and to have these so-called "secret police" standing right out in the open would be the best early warning system that Stalin, the one-time weatherman, could have ever had.

As his train approached the observatory, Stalin saw the army of police standing outside waiting for him. He simply decided not to get off at his stop. Stalin stayed on for the ride, and in that split second determined to ditch his gig and as a part-time meteorologist in order to become a full-time revolutionary.

Chapter Two

The Real Revolution Begins

"Everybody has a right to be stupid, but some people abuse the privilege."

—Joseph Stalin

Shortly after his leave from the Tiflis Meteorological Observatory, Joseph Stalin's true education into Marxism began. It was around this time that several radical Russian exiles, imbued with the teachings of Karl Marx, began to flood onto the scene, injecting their ideology in the robust worker's movements of Tiflis and other frontier towns. One of these new political dissidents to enter the Georgian fold was a man by the name of Mikhail Ivanovich Kalinin.

It would be Kalinin that would later help forge the revolutionary structure with Stalin and Lenin. Right at the turn of the century, when he first came into Stalin's awareness, however, he was simply one of many exiles who sought to establish a strong base for the Russian Social-Democratic Labor Party (RSDLP) in the region.

The RSLDP was a revolutionary political party that was formed in 1898. It was in the summer of 1901 that Stalin was persuaded to join the party, it was shortly after this that he was sent out of Tiflis to Btumi , another frontier town, in which he finally stepped out of the shadows and sought to define himself more clearly within the social democratic movement.

As Stalin gained more and more notoriety, he also gained more attention from the secret police. This made the obscure auspices of Btumi, just 12 miles from the Turkish border, a much safer haven for the revolution. It was to here, right on the edge of what was left of the old Ottoman Empire, that Stalin embarked. This was a highly diverse region filled with Georgians, Kurds, and Turks. It was also an industrial hub with several big factories, mills, and plants.

Here, Stalin would unleash a series of massively effective strikes, completely shutting down major facilities, including the Rothschild Oil Refinery. It was this refinery strike that would go down as one of Stalin's crowning achievements in subversion; in his scheme to take out this vital resource of the Russian Empire, Stalin actually took a job at the plant, pretending to be just an average day laborer at the facility.

It wasn't long before Stalin began agitating and calling on his fellow workers to rise up against the plant's owners. In one particularly dramatic moment of the strike, Stalin is said to have encouraged his comrades by shouting, "We mustn't fear death! The sun is rising! Let's sacrifice or lives!"

Stalin believed that they were on the verge of something great and the sun would soon rise to a brand new day of revolution. Stalin and others then attempted to set the whole refinery on fire, but this attempt was prevented by several other concerned workers on the scene. After all of the commotion, the wrath of the local authorities would finally strike back on March 7th, 1902.

Stalin managed to escape their initial dragnet, but several of his fellow strike leaders were arrested. Unfazed, Stalin boldly formed demonstrations right outside of the police headquarters, demanding that the arrested leaders be released. As more police began to encircle the crowd, things began to get ugly on both sides, and fearing that they would be arrested regardless, the crowd decided to make an attempt at storming the prison in order to forcefully free their comrades.

Realizing the gravity of the situation, the police called in additional reinforcements in the form of Cossack troops, who quickly helped turn the tide against Stalin and his revolutionary demonstrators. In all, after the conflict drew to a close, 15 lay dead, 54 were horribly wounded, and 500 were sent off to prison - which in those days usually meant a trip to the frigid, northernmost region of the Russian Empire: Siberia.

Stalin was one of those 500 and would begin a long exile in the land of frost and snow, through whose coldness he would first craft for himself his identity as the "Man of Steel," changing his name from Josif Dzhugashvili to *Joseph Stalin*. It was also during his first stint in Siberia that he made contact with Vladimir Lenin, the man who would come to found the first official communist party of Russia.

While the men did not yet get the opportunity to speak face to face, Lenin had heard of Stalin's exploits, and with Lenin himself being a prolific writer, began to communicate with him through a series of letters. Stalin was very much impressed with Lenin's intellect and his plans for transforming Russia into a communist state. This was the moment that Stalin was completely converted from being a populist rabble-rouser to a full blown communist revolutionary under Lenin's guidance.

Egged on by Lenin's encouragement, Stalin would manage to pull off a daring escape from his Siberian prison on January 5th, 1904. He would find his way back to Georgia in February; during this period Stalin continued to stay low, but even in this state of perpetual hiding he managed to meet and marry his first wife, Ekaterina Svanidze, in 1906. They would have a son named Yakov one year later.

Instead of settling down to family life, however, Stalin increased his revolutionary ambition, adding bank robbery to his list of subversive activities. It was on June 26th, 1907 that Stalin would pull off what would became known as the infamous "Tiflis Bank Robbery," in which he and a gang of collaborators ambushed an armored convoy carrying a bank cash shipment to the Imperial Bank of Russia of what would be the equivalent of millions of U.S. dollars.

Stalin and his compatriots swooped down on the main stagecoach of the convoy, encircling the armed guards and police escorting the money. A desperate firefight then broke out that would leave over forty dead and fifty severely injured. Before further reinforcements arrived, Stalin and his crew managed to escape with over 341,000

Russian Rubles, which would be about 3.4 million U.S. dollars today.

Although many in the party hailed this brazen move as a heroic modern version of Robin Hood, with the noble Marxists redistributing the government-controlled wealth of the corrupt capitalists back to the cause of the common people, others did not take too kindly to armed robbery and murder committed under the banner of the Russian Social Democratic Party.

This split of opinion is what would lead to a schism between the Bolsheviks (Russian for "the Majority") led by Lenin and Stalin, and the so-called Mensheviks, (Russian for "the Minority") led by the rest, who disapproved of such strong-arm tactics. However, among the Bolsheviks, the robbery only served to bolster Stalin's reputation as a man of action, and his reputation among the revolutionaries was greatly enhanced as a result.

The life of an avid revolutionary may not have been the most conducive for families, however, and in the midst of his zealous involvement his wife contracted a bad case of typhus, eventually passing away on December 5th, 1907. In the aftermath, Joseph Stalin, the Man of Steel, found himself in the throes of the most horrible of human grief. Despite his proclaimed exterior of metal, his heart ached horribly for the love he had lost, and, as he confided in one of his close friends at the time, "with her died my last warm feeling for humanity."

Chapter Three

From Exile to Supreme Leader

"It's not the people who vote that count. It's the people who count the votes."

—Joseph Stalin

In the ten years between 1907 and 1917, Stalin would be arrested and exiled to Siberia on four separate occasions. With the exception of his fourth exile, Stalin always found a way to escape. The seeming ease with which Stalin broke free from his imprisonment led some to speculate that he must have had help from the inside, but there isn't any real proof to lend credence to such claims.

Many have pointed out that despite the harshness of the Siberian terrain, the region was poorly guarded and escape attempts were quite common. For someone with the audacity and sheer determination of Stalin, a pilgrimage for freedom through even the harshest of Siberian winters would not be that hard to believe. It was during his fourth and final stint in exile that Europe erupted into the flames that would become World War One.

Even though Stalin had been exiled from the Russian Empire as a treacherous revolutionary, the Tsar still needed as many troops as he could muster, and so it was that Stalin was pulled out of the gulag in 1916 for conscription into the Russian army. But when he was then taken to Krasnoyarsk, the largest outpost in southern Siberia for a medical checkup, the examiner took note of his damaged left arm and deemed him unfit for military service.

Stalin would later remember this event with grim satisfaction, knowing that the very arm that other children had used to ruthlessly tease him about growing up very well could have saved him from being killed in the trenches, fighting for a country he didn't even believe in. Deemed practically useless to the Russian army, Stalin was sent back to the gulag, where he would stay for the remainder of the war.

While he languished in exile, the Russian government would become increasingly desperate during the war effort. From the beginning, the Russian military was too outdated and ill-equipped to effectively fight against its opponents in the conflict. Due to a massive arms shortage, several soldiers were even sent to the front lines without weapons, instructed to just pick up whatever discarded guns they could find in the trenches.

Meanwhile, Germany and its Ottoman allies succeeded in mounting a complete blockade of all Russian supplies coming in through the Black and Baltic Seas. This led to massive fuel and food shortages that made life for the average Russian increasingly miserable.

Massive civil unrest in the form of strikes and protests soon spread throughout the Russian Empire, reaching a fever pitch until the Tsarist regime, under the vice grip of international and internal turmoil, finally collapsed altogether in February 1917. As soon as Vladimir Lenin heard the news he returned from his own self-imposed exile in Germany to finally implement his vision of a communist revolution.

Before he could address the internal discord of his country, however, he had to craft a solution for the international discord that still raged in the trenches for World War One. With no reason to fight the Tsar's war any longer, Lenin immediately reached out to the Central powers of Europe (Germany, Austro-Hungary, and the Ottoman Empire) and sued them for peace.

It was from this that the Treaty of Brest-Litovsk was fashioned, in which a cessation of hostilities was granted at the high price of the loss of nearly all of Russia's satellite nations, such as Ukraine and other Baltic states. Southern territory, such as Western Armenia, was also ceded to the Ottomans.

As harsh as the terms of the treaty were for the newly established Soviet Government, their effects would prove to be very brief. In May of 1918, when Germany surrendered to the Allied Powers the treaty was made completely null and void. Meanwhile, in the middle of all of this international intrigue, Joseph Stalin found a new role for himself in the new Soviet system in his appointment as "People's Commissar for Nationalities Affairs."

It was here that Stalin the revolutionary and insurrectionist would first learn how to be a politician, as Commissar Stalin had to shoulder, for the first time, the political organization of a vast amount of people. It was essentially Stalin's first real taste of leadership. It was shortly after this appointment that a bloody civil war broke out between Lenin's Red Army and the so-called White Army, which was composed of anti-Bolshevik militants.

It was during this period that Lenin would form an initial Politburo consisting of five members: Lenin himself, Leon Trotsky, Lev Kamenev, Nikolai Krestinksy, and Joseph Stalin. This was one of many hats that Stalin already wore; as a result of this position, Stalin was sent to the city of Tsaritsyn, the town that would eventually become "Stalingrad." where he was first given authority to exert his control over the Russian army.

One of the first measures that Stalin had carried out in his reorganization of the military was to have many of the former officers of the Tsar shot and killed. Stalin sought to defeat any attempt to bring back the Tsarist government by snuffing out the most distinguished officers from the regime. His efforts only served to escalate matters, however, and soon all of Russia was in the grip of a brutal civil war between the newly established Red Army and the White Army of the old regime.

The White Army and its remnants of governance were then bolstered by a series of expeditions by the British, Americans, Italians and Japanese, who sought to interfere and foil the communist takeover. All of these efforts of support would be futile, however, and by 1921 the White Army was defeated. As recognition of some of Stalin's early successes in organizing the Red Army, in 1922 Lenin gave Stalin the post of General Secretary.

At this time, the post merely served the role of party administration, a position used to determine party membership. Stalin would later transform this title to mean much, much more. Shortly after Lenin appointed Stalin as General Secretary, he suffered from a series of strokes. His health rapidly deteriorated after this and, becoming paralyzed in his left arm and leg, he was soon bedridden and unable to attend official meetings.

It seems that while Lenin was on his very deathbed, he began to have some serious misgivings about Stalin and wrote long letters criticizing everything from his harsh political views to his rude manners. Lenin then began to tell anyone who would listen to him that Stalin should be removed from the position of General Secretary immediately.

When Lenin finally died on January 21st, 1924, a power struggle soon followed. In this struggle Stalin's main opponent was Trotsky. Despite Lenin's warning about Stalin, to the rest of the Politburo Stalin seemed like the more conservative choice for his commitment to the consolidation of power, whereas Trotsky seemed too extreme in his desire to spark multiple outside communist revolutions.

Although Stalin would eventually win out in the court of popular opinion and be unanimously voted into office, he also realized just how easily he could have been voted out and continued to see Trotsky as his ultimate threat. Trotsky also continued to criticize Stalin's policies for suppressing democracy in the communist party. As a result, Stalin launched a vicious propaganda campaign against Trotsky to ruin his reputation among officials.

The campaign was successful and resulted in his removal from his position as the "War Commissariat." As accusations against him continued to mount, he would be ejected from the Communist Party completely by 1927. Trotsky's fall would prove to be a precipitous one, and by 1928 he was banned from the Soviet Union altogether, forced to go into hiding on the Turkish island of Prinkipo.

Trotsky would never return. His exile would be a permanent one, eventually leading to his assassination in 1940. Stalin, with his political foes silenced and removed, began to consolidate his power base even more, making sure he would never be threatened ever again and that no one would question the right of the Man of Steel, Joseph Stalin, to reign supreme.

Chapter Four

A Brave New Word

"The death of one man is tragic, but the death of thousands is a statistic."

—Joseph Stalin

With his enemies shut down or otherwise on the run, Stalin set about rebuilding his Soviet Empire. He always felt that the Russian state was terribly backward when compared to its European and American counterparts; Stalin felt that it was up to him to leapfrog his nation ahead of the rest, and he intended to do it through his incredibly ambitious "Five Year Plan."

The Five Rear Plan was a specific list of industrial and economic policy goals that Stalin created and sought to complete between the five-year span of 1928 to 1932. A major part of this plan was the collective farming systems that Stalin enacted in 1929. Russia had been, in previous centuries, much more agrarian than it was industrial. Farms were the lifeblood of the Russian peasants, and many farmers had lived self-sufficiently for many years.

After Stalin had issued his edict of pooling all resources and farmlands together in the collective greater good of communism, these rugged individuals who were used to pulling their own weight for themselves were thrown into chaos. Many of the disgruntled farmers killed their animals and stored the meat for themselves, and hid additional crops rather than giving it all up to the collective.

When word got back to Stalin of their interference, it did not bode well. He immediately sent out teams of Government Enforcers to make sure that everyone was equally submitting their resources. Secret police would show up announced at a farmer's house and then proceed to ransack the place in search of hidden produce. Those who did not cooperate lost everything and were sent immediately to the gulags of Siberia.

As the work camps of Siberia swelled, Stalin was granted with another resource that he would use to rapidly industrialize the Soviet Union: slave labor. Over the next five years, he would use the thousands of prisoners working at breakneck speeds to achieve industrial projects on a grand scale. Soon, massive centers of industry emerged in previously backwater areas of such as Magnitogorsk, Dnieper, and Nizhny Novgorod.

Nizhny Novgorod, in particular, became a very important automobile plant that would soon mass produce vast amounts of cars in an incredibly short period of time. This would come as a delight of Soviet citizens, most of whom had never driven a car before. With industrial wonders such as Nizhny Novgorod, it can not be denied that Stalin was able to achieve major milestones of industrialization in a short period of time.

During a scant five years, the entire industrial output of the Soviet Union would be increased by 50 percent. Russian national income rose from 24.4 to 96.3 Russian

Rubles during this time as well. However, no matter what the short-term payout was, the cost of this great leap forward would be absolutely staggering when it came to human life, with hundreds of thousands of workers meeting their deaths from starvation, exhaustion, and abuse by their vicious state-sanctioned overseers.

It was Stalin's version of building the pyramids, and just like the Pharaoh of old, he quite literally worked his people to death in order to achieve his monumental vision of what he believed Soviet Russia should be. As brutal as Stalin's measures were, however, it would prove vitally necessary in order for his people to be able to stand up and fend off a brand new threat coming from the west, a resurging Germany led by a dictator that was even more ruthless than Stalin.

Joseph Stalin's first dealings with Adolf Hitler came in the form of secret trade deals in which Berlin allowed the Soviet Union to purchase a limited amount of military equipment. The relationship between Germany and the Soviet Union, from Hitler's rise in 1933 and the Nazi invasion of Russia in 1941, was a strange and at times bizarre dance. From the outset, Hitler's fascist National Socialism was anathema to Stalin's communist supposed ideals for a Soviet Russia.

Yet these two men, in their personal makeup, were not so different from each other. They were both bitterly hardened men who demanded that their subjects revere them as god-like figures, and they both would stop at nothing to ensure their absolute, tyrannical rule. Both of these men also realized that they would probably have to face each other in battle someday, their diametrically opposed views and powerful interests in Central Europe made this an almost certain reality.

These two infamous dictators continued their game of chess, each one watching the other as they carefully made their move. Although he viewed Hitler's Germany as a future source of conflict, Stalin preferred to play it safe. In 1933, at the time of Hitler's emergence on the world stage, even though the Soviets had just completed their first massive, national industrial project—the five-year plan—Stalin felt that being pulled into a major conflict with Germany would be disastrous.

Deciding that the Soviet Union still needed a few more years to modernize its military before it could ever challenge Germany on an equal footing, Stalin decided it would be best to forestall and delay the inevitable aggression of Nazi Germany. In the meantime, Stalin attempted to make overtures to those he thought would keep Germany in check, the Western powers of France and Britain.

Seeking to encircle the belligerent Germans by aligning the Soviet Union with these two Western Democracies, Stalin thought that the German militancy could be held at bay. However, Britain and France, mostly viewing Stalin and his communist regime with abhorrence, turned a deaf ear to his suggestions. Stalin was especially frustrated in 1938 when he was apparently not invited to the party that would become the "Munich Agreement."

Resulting from Hitler bullying his way into Czechoslovakia under the absurd claim that he was protecting "German speakers" who lived in the countryside of the nation's southern border, the Munich Agreement was an appeasement to Hitler that allowed him to annex vast tracts of Czechoslovakia, which he renamed the "Sudetenland," into his German regime.

While this Central European land was being carved up like a piece of pie for the Germans, the Soviets, who were themselves under special agreements such as the "mutual military assistance treaty" with Czechoslovakia, weren't even brought in to discuss the process. This was too much for Stalin, and this was the point in which he finally gave up on any meaningful dialogue with Britain and France over the German question and instead decided to openly engage the Germans himself.

Meanwhile, the Czechoslovakians were appalled at the fact that their land and people were being bartered away to the Germans without anyone making any effort to help them stand for their own rights as a sovereign nation. Taking the hint, the Soviets—instead of waiting for a British proclamation or a French go-between—decided to take matters into their own hands by engaging the Germans directly. These efforts would eventually materialize into the infamous "Molotov-Ribbentrop Pact" of 1939.

This pact, signed by the two countries' foreign ministers, would lock the pair of nations into a neutral non-aggression pact. On the surface, this document was just a simple statement of professed neutrality, but delve deeper into the treaty, and you find the secret provisions that guaranteed whole-scale division of Eastern Europe into Soviet and German domains of influence.

At Stalin's behest, the German's had promised to give the Soviets a free hand in Eastern Poland, Finland, Estonia, Romania, and Latvia, as long as the Russians did not interfere with their "other" military ambitions. With the ink barely dry on the agreement, the Germans then stormed into western Poland, leading Britain and France to both declare war on the Nazis.

Just two weeks later, Stalin would send his own Red Army into Eastern Poland to take his share of the Polish nation that the "non-aggression" pact had allotted him, essentially making it a joint Nazi/Soviet offensive that crushed the Poles from both sides. Interestingly enough, even though the British and French didn't hesitate to declare war on Nazi Germany, they never declared war on the Russians, even though their initial invasion and occupation of Eastern Poland were just as brutal as the Nazi invasions of Western Poland.

Most analysts would argue that this was sheer pragmatism on the part of these Western countries since they sensed that having to fight off both the German war machine and an endless flow of Soviet troops would have been impossible. Perhaps this was what Hitler had hoped for when the non-aggression pact with Stalin had been connived in the first place.

He most likely would have been very pleased if his initial attack on Poland could have dragged Brittan and France into a knock-down, drag-out fight with the Soviets as well as the Germans. However, putting the ethics of their pledges to protect Poland from "all enemies" aside, Britain and France pointedly chose to focus primarily on the Germans occupying the western half of Poland while ignoring those that threatened the Poles of the east.

Britain would soon have much more to worry about. The Germans managed to crush France in a stunning blitzkrieg attack, defeating them in a matter of days. Under such conditions, a confrontation with Stalin for his own role in the Polish conflict would not be forthcoming. For the British, with the Germans now staring them down from occupied France's shores, the threat of Stalin's domination in Eastern Europe would have to wait.

Chapter Five

Stalin's Gambit

"In war I would deal with the Devil and his grandmother."

—Joseph Stalin

By most accounts, Stalin was genuinely surprised on June 22nd, 1941 when his "non-aggression" pact partner Adolf Hitler launched an invasion of the Soviet Union. When Russia entered into its backroom deals with Germany, it was simply a means to an end. Stalin felt that war in Europe would be inevitable, but he was working a long game in which he hoped that Germany, England, and France would fight each other to a standstill in a protracted struggle, completely exhausting their resources. Meanwhile, he would work to build up tremendous resources for the Soviets, allowing them to emerge at the end of the conflict with a fresh and vastly more powerful army that could easily subdue the weakened belligerents.

When Hitler managed to conquer France in just a few weeks without expending hardly any resources at all, Stalin began to have second thoughts about his grand scheme. According to the man who would one day succeed him, Nikita Khrushchev recalled just how downcast and agitated Stalin had become when he first heard of Germany's surprising victories in the field.

According to Khrushchev, Stalin, in one of his particularly disgusted moods, had "cursed the French for letting themselves by beaten" and claimed that the British were "fleeing as fast as their legs could carry them."

When Hitler finally tore through Soviet territory on June 22nd, 1941, despite the writing already being on the wall, Stalin for all intents and purposes appeared to be in a state of shock. At first, he absolutely refused to accept the reality of the invasion. He kept telling his associates that there must be some sort of mistake, that perhaps the attacks were the result of a rogue Nazi general and refused to believe that Hitler had just started a war against the Soviet Union.

Amazingly, in his search for answers, contrary to the hard reality of full blown German attack, he even had his Foreign Ministry Office reach out to Germany's ally Japan in a vain attempt to mediate through what he insisted was just a misunderstanding with the Axis power. Despite Stalin's unusual and highly uncharacteristic display of magnanimous restraint when it came to the Germans, no mediation would be forthcoming. While the German war machine rapidly advanced, Stalin became unresponsive to his colleagues, isolating himself and refusing to attend official meetings for days at a time.

Meanwhile, the Red Army was in a state of complete discord, as so many valuable Generals and intelligence officers had been executed in Stalin's purge of just a few years before that the command structure of the military was nearly non-existent. Now that Soviet troops found themselves facing off against the highly efficient and organized German military, they were being cut down like grass. Communication behind Soviet lines was a mess, and whole divisions became lost simply trying to find the enemy.

The situation seemed so despairingly bleak that Stalin lost yet another of his top Generals—this time to suicide—when Major General Nikolai Vashigin shot himself in the head right in front of them. As Germany made increasing gains, Stalin himself grew even more belligerent and inconsolable; at one meeting party members recall him simply storming out of the conference room shouting in a surprisingly raw show of self-deprecating despair, "Lenin founded our state and now we've f*****it up!"

Stalin was in a terrible position. It was his darkest midnight hour, and he began to doubt his own judgment. Did he really just undo all of the gains that he and Lenin believed had made for the Soviet Union? The Man of Steel had finally been crushed by the pressure he himself had helped to build up. After this testy exchange at the Politburo Stalin again went into isolation, locking himself in his house. When he didn't appear at the next meeting, his officials forced their way into his home to find their great leader in a state of abject depression and anxiety.

Instead of defiantly demanding why they were intruding on him at his personal quarters like he might have done in the past, a much less confident Stalin simply looked up at his guests and asked in a trembling voice, "Why—why have you come?" Stalin seemed completely beside himself, but the answer from his foreign minister Molotov was simple: "we're asking you to return to work."

In his moment of severe doubt, Stalin seemed genuinely surprised that anyone would still look to him for leadership after his failure to prepare for the German attack.

His officers who found him in this dejected state of disillusion would later assert their impression that Stalin believed they had come to arrest him. In that instant, Stalin had succumbed to his worst fears and believed that the ruthless apparatus he had painstakingly constructed to root out the traitors and the weak had finally turned on him as the most treacherous and weakest of all.

But his loyal followers did not arrest their leader and send him to be tortured in the gulags for his failure. Instead, they rallied behind him in hopes that the Man of Steel that they had known in the past could make a return and somehow save their nation from destruction at the hands of the Germans.

On July 3, 1941, Stalin would deliver a rousing and heartfelt speech to the people of the Soviet Union. In this speech he spoke directly to the Soviet citizen, calling them his brothers and sisters and even his "friends," urging them to rise up against the German enemy that wished to enslave them and take away their freedom.

Amazingly, in the midst of the crisis, Stalin's persuasive gambit would pay off, even though he himself had waged terror on his own people and repressed their freedoms for many years. The Soviet citizenry began to agree with him and saw the struggle with the Germans as a very fight for their existence.

They believed Stalin when he informed them that "the enemy is cruel and implacable. He is out to seize our lands which have been watered by the sweat of our brow, to seize our grain and oil which have been obtained by the labor of our hands. He is out to restore the rule of the landlords, to restore tsarism, to destroy the national culture and the national existence of the Russians and the other free peoples of the Soviet Union, to Germanize them, to convert them into the slaves of German princes and barons."

Soon after his powerful address, millions of Soviet subjects who had most likely never even heard his voice before were suddenly electrified and ready to die for their country - and for Stalin. In his gamble as to whether or not his people would lay down their lives for him in this gambit in his long game against the Germans would prove to be tragically correct.

Chapter Six

Stalin Makes a Comeback

"Great Britain provided time; the United States provided money, and Soviet Russia provided blood."

—Joseph Stalin

As the year 1941 drew to a close, the Soviet Union had already suffered 4.3 million deaths in a war that was only a few months old. To put that figure into perspective, at the ending of all hostilities during World War Two, the United States had lost a total of about 400,000 soldiers, and that was over a period of roughly three and a half years from December 1941 to August 1945.

Compare that to the four million Soviets who were dead in just a couple of months. Stalin kept urging his ill-prepared flock forward to their German slaughterers. By the end of World War Two, a mind-boggling 20 million Soviets would lay dead, the greatest death toll of any participant in the war, with no other country even coming close. Soviet blood would come to perpetually stain the fields of Russia.

During this tremendous loss of life, Nazi propagandists took note of the severe price that was being paid by the Russians and actively worked to use the massive death toll against Stalin, dropping thousands of leaflets with slogans such as "Do not shed your blood for

Stalin!" imprinted on the front, but such tactics of persuasion mostly fell on deaf ears. The Russians, as ill-equipped as they were, would fight on as the Nazis tore deeper and deeper into their land.

By September 8th, 1941, the Germans had Leningrad (previously St. Petersburg) completely surrounded. Hitler, wishing to save resources, did not order an invasion but prolonged the misery of the city's residents by forcing them into submission through a combination of constant bombing from the Luftwaffe and through the sheer starvation of its blockaded people.

Harkening all the way back to medieval times when armies would wage wars of attrition against walled cities, the siege of Leningrad would become the longest duration of siege warfare to ever take place in any modern city. And as Hitler had predicted, the people of Leningrad were starving to death just a couple of months later in November.

In total, more than a million Soviets would perish from a combination of hunger, disease, aerial bombardment, and intermittent gunfire. When word had reached Moscow of the desperate plight of the denizens of Leningrad, Stalin did what he did best in times of crisis: he formed a committee. He held a conference with his commanders about what it might take to turn the war around.

In particular, he asked an up and coming leader of the Red Army named Georgy Zhukov what resources would need to be procured from the central planning apparatus of the communist system. Fortunately for Stalin, Zhukov knew exactly what he needed from his Soviet Santa Claus and immediately requested brand new tanks, artillery, and rockets to be assembled on the massive Marxist assembly lines.

After taking note of the request, Stalin then turned to Zhukov and asked him bluntly, "Tell me, Georgy, as a Communist to a fellow Communist, are we going to hold Moscow or not?" Zhukov, without hesitation responded to his chairman, "Comrade Stalin, if I get even part of the help that I asked for, we will hold Moscow." Amazingly, this conversation was all it took for Stalin the master organizer to ignite the furnace of Soviet industry. Using all the totalitarian power at his command, he forced his factories to pump out armaments like there was no tomorrow.

For the industrial centers of the farther eastern reaches of the Soviet Union, it was no problem to begin massive production quotas; the development of the product was not the issue. The main obstacle was figuring out how to transfer equipment once it was produced. When it came to Leningrad in particular, opening up a supply line to the besieged city became of paramount importance.

After much maneuvering, a corridor was finally established by traveling over the southern part of Lake Ladoga just to the east of Leningrad. This was carried out first by boat over the water and then with armored trucks and other land transport vehicles over the thick frozen ice of the winter months, which created a reliable ice road directly into the city. This route also became an essential backdoor out of the city for those who were allowed to evacuate.

The word "allowed" has to be stressed, because the Russian secret police had strict orders to prevent mass desertion of the city and only allowed a few civilians to leave. Sadly, this meant the residents of Leningrad were being held hostage on two fronts: by the advancing Nazis and by their own Soviet enforcers.

From the beginning, Stalin was determined to bring severe law and order to the Russian populace, and in his bid to keep his people from all-out panic he ordered teams of NKVD agents to shoot citizens on sight if they were perceived to be disrupting that order. Tragically, for most of those who lived in Leningrad, there would be no escape, and death would come in the form of slow starvation.

According to official records, every resident was rationed out a mere 1/3rd of a pound of bread, which amounted to just a handful of breadcrumbs mixed with sawdust and dirt. This meager sustenance was all that was available the first year of the siege, and after 1942 even this ration was often unavailable, leaving people to improvise the best they could.

The stories of these improvisations are wide-ranging, with tales of survival by eating grass or even roving bands of kids catching stray cats for a meal. The worst stories, however, started to circulate during the harsh winter month of December 1941, when the secret police started to receive reports of cannibalism. It is hard to know how many of these stories were simply anecdotal rumor and how many reflected a much more gruesome reality.

The NKVD has on record the arrest of 2,105 people who were accused of all-out cannibalism. These cases were categorized by those who simply ate the flesh of people who had already died and those who actively murdered their victims for the sole purpose of eating them.

It was this scene out of a horror movie that the Soviet citizens of Leningrad lived under until their freedom finally came in January of 1944 when a major Soviet offensive finally pushed the Germans back. Before the Germans were finally driven off, however, Stalin had to deal with an offensive even closer to home as the Germans threatened to break down the very gates of Moscow.

Chapter Seven

Defending the Capitol

"We don't let them have ideas. Why would we let them have guns?"

—Joseph Stalin

In the final months of 1941, Moscow appeared to be in an increasingly precarious position. Called "Operation Typhoon," the German dash to Moscow began on November 15th, 1941, and in just five days the Germans were only 20 miles away from downtown Moscow. This was actually close enough for long range Nazi guns to take potshots at the Kremlin.

The Germans hoped that this would help terrorize the citizens and shake the Russian leadership to know that they were in the line of fire. Stalin had now shaken off his initial malaise and was personally seeing to the defense of Moscow himself. Stalin, positioning himself to be the living embodiment of his people's will to go on, now worked to present himself as the Soviet champion who would answer the cruelty and harshness of the Germans with harshness of his own.

In one rather candid and rousing speech on November 6th, 1941, he didn't mince words, explaining to the citizens of Moscow exactly what was at stake against the genocidal armies of Nazi Germany. Answering their brutality with his firm resolve, he declared, "If the Germans want a war of extermination, they shall have one."

He then highlighted the reasons why he believed it would be the invading Germans that would be on the receiving end of that extermination. Speaking to the populace as if they were his family, he then sought to remind them that the "Soviet Family" had been through worse before, highlighting the desperate condition of the Red Army in 1918 shortly after the revolution.

Stalin then sought to transmit his confidence that even with Germans surrounding the outskirts of Moscow the balance would shift in their favor. Unbeknownst to most of his listeners, however, Stalin's own confidence had been recently bolstered from a steady stream of intelligence reports he had been receiving in regard to Japan.

As it turns out, Stalin had been saving some of his best troops for last. Holed up in the far reaches of Siberia where a supply of fresh crack troops that had previously been positioned in the Far East to stave off a potential invasion from the Japanese. For several weeks, however, his agents in East Asia had been informing him that Japanese plans for a Soviet invasion had been scrapped, and the Imperial army of Japan would instead focus on the Pacific.

With the threat of being squeezed in two different directions at once by Japan and Germany taken off the table, Stalin could tell his people with confidence that the German threat would soon be dealt with once and for all. On December 7th, 1941, Japan launched a surprise attack on the United States, proving that the intelligence reports he had been receiving were correct.

Reassured and comforted by this knowledge, Stalin unleashed his ferocious horde from Siberia. Stalin sent these hardened fighters, who excelled battling in harsh winter elements, to intercept the German forces on the outskirts of Moscow. Hitler's troops were already exhausted, frostbitten, and half-delirious from the cold; they were no match for these hardened Siberian combatants who thrived in the ice and snow.

The Nazis were quickly pushed back 50 miles further from Moscow, marking Germany's very first major defeat of World War Two. This defeat caused Hitler to change his tactics, and instead of seeking a crushing defeat against Stalin, he would seek resources to further fuel his war machine. Those resources lay in the oil-rich fields of the Southern Caucasus.

All Soviet intelligence pointed to this change of directives as well, but Stalin refused to believe it and instead remained convinced that the battle for Moscow wasn't over. He refused to send reinforcements to the south. As a result, without additional support, the Germans were able to decimate the isolated Soviet divisions positioned in the Caucasus. With the Caucasian Mountains in their grasp, the Germans then moved on to Stalingrad.

The city of Stalingrad in itself had no strategic importance, but Hitler just couldn't resist laying siege to the town that bore the name of his nemesis. Succumbing once again to his greatest weakness of putting symbolism before pragmatism, Hitler had locked his soldiers in a vicious battle to the death on the streets of the city.

The German effort to take Stalingrad began in earnest in August of 1942 when the German 6th Army, bolstered by part of the 4th Panzer Army and even some divisions lent from the Nazi ally of Romania, moved on the city. With massive Luftwaffe bombing overhead, the Germans stormed into the urban landscape and began bitter and costly house-to-house fighting.

Initially, the Soviet soldiers were driven back, but on July 28th, 1942, Stalin would issue his "Not One Step Back" policy and order his men to hold their lines and fight the Germans. After fanatic fighting on both sides, the Germans slowly began to push the Soviets back until they occupied only a 9-mile radius along the Volga River. It was this river that had been the city's original namesake; it had been called "Volgograd" before Stalin decided to name the southern industrial hub after himself.

In this time of dire need, it would be the Volga River that would prove crucial in keeping its Soviet defense alive. The beleaguered troops' only source of supplies would come to them by means of a riverboat barge. By October 14th, the German advance threatened to shut down even this vital lifeline; the Soviets were nearly pushed into the river itself, fighting for dear life under heavy artillery fire.

The German high command believed that Stalingrad would soon fall, but Stalin himself had other plans. On November 19th, he ordered a major counterstrike to be directed under General Zhukov in which two Soviet divisions were hurled at the weakest points of the Axis line, smashing into armies mostly composed of less well trained and less motivated Romanian, Italian, and Hungarian soldiers.

By November 23rd these lines were broken, and the Soviets managed to completely encircle the Germans, who were still entrenched within Stalingrad. Knowing the desperate position that they were in, Hitler's generals continuously requested permission to have the surrounded forces mount a charge to break through the circle and retreat back to the west of Stalingrad.

Hitler, as stubborn as ever, refused, insisting that every man should "stand and fight." The trapped Germans grew weaker as the Russian winter grew colder; by December, they were nearly out of food and supplies. At this point, even the belligerence of Hitler had to realize that without help some of his best divisions within Stalingrad would be devastated.

In a last ditch effort to save face, he enacted Operation Winter Tempest, in which a new division of Germans was sent to break the Soviet line and fight their way east through the city to the trapped German fighters. The Volga River was now frozen solid, however, making it the perfect ice road for Soviet equipment and fighters to pour through the city.

By February 1943 the situation for the Germans was absolutely hopeless. The German troops who remained had hands that were so frostbitten they could barely even pull the triggers of their guns. Faced with such overwhelming odds, the Germans had no choice but to surrender, making Stalingrad, the city with such symbolic meaning for both Stalin and Hitler, the first major turning point in the war. The tide of the war would now inevitably turn westward until the Red Army stormed into Berlin itself, allowing Stalin's ambition of a communist-dominated Europe to become a reality.

Chapter Eight

Going West

"In the Soviet army it takes more courage to retreat than advance."

—Joseph Stalin

Joseph Stalin had previously been rebuffed and virtually ignored by the Allied war effort against Hitler. Some would even argue that it was the cold shoulder of the West that caused Stalin to turn to Germany for a "nonaggression" pact in the first place. However, now with the German army decisively crushed at Stalingrad, it would be the West that would seek out Stalin who at this point—one year before the Americans would even attempt D-Day—was the only world leader to so decisively beat back the Nazi threat.

It was in a state of victorious exuberance that Stalin first sat down at the table with his supposed Western allies on November 28th, 1943 in Tehran, Iran for the first of the so-called "Big Three" peace talks to discuss the Allied plan for the postwar world. Sitting next to American President Franklin Delano Roosevelt and British Prime Minister Winston Churchill, Stalin felt like he was in a prime position to dictate the terms.

Britain was weary and shaken from heavy losses; the United States, fresh to the fold, was rather naïve when it came to the threat of communist domination. Adding to this was the string of Soviet victories over the enemy that gave Stalin the clout he needed to make his demands. First, Stalin insisted that the allies open a second front against the Germans through France.

This had at this point been delayed in favor of attacking the Axis' soft underbelly through North Africa and Italy. However, with Stalin's impressive gains in the East, the Allies realized that they needed to act and agreed to mount an amphibious assault on the western shores of German-occupied Europe. The second demand that Stalin would make would be for the domination of Eastern Europe itself.

Stalin drove a hard bargain; he demanded that the Soviet Union's border be pushed out all the way to Eastern Poland. Amazingly both the U.S. and Britain agreed to these strong terms out of their desperate need for Stalin to take on the Germans. Not too pleased with the idea of having to explain to the Polish why they had just given away the eastern half of their country, Roosevelt and Churchill came up with the idea of giving Poland part of Western Germany as a sort of divvied up consolation prize.

It was the last gasp attempt to ameliorate the consequences of the Soviets having a free hand in Europe, but in reality, even this dismal attempt at fairness would never come into play. Once the Soviets marched into Berlin, the frontiers of the Soviet Empire would not only encompass Poland but would take East Germany itself into the Soviet Bloc as well.

The Nazi regime would make its final stand against Stalin's armies in April of 1945, when 1.9 million German soldiers, hopelessly depleted of ammunition, energy, and hope faced off against a resurgent and energized Red Army that was 6.4 million strong. The Soviets quickly made short work of this pathetic defense force, and on May 2nd they made their way right to the heart of Berlin. Stalin had ordered his men to search for Hitler, but unbeknownst to Stalin, he was already dead from a self-inflicted gunshot wound.

Although Stalin's intelligence officers immediately informed him of the suicide, Stalin would continuously insinuate over the next few years that Hitler had most likely escaped and was still alive somewhere. Many believe that Stalin was using this disinformation as a propaganda tool against Britain and the United States. Stalin believed that if he could keep his Western rivals focused on the ghost of Hitler long enough, he could keep them from paying too much attention to his own dealings.

Regardless of the obscurity of Hitler's demise, Nazi Germany came to a full and unconditional surrender on May 7th, 1945. On this day Americans, Britons, and Russians alike celebrated their hard-won victory. The Soviet Union, taking special pride in its critical role in Germany's defeat launched a series of extravagant celebrations in order to honor their brave military personnel, and of course to honor their supreme leader, Joseph Stalin.

Most famously, a massive victory parade was launched in Red Square on June 24th, 1945. It was originally intended for Stalin to lead the parade, but at the last minute, plans were changed, and it was determined that the most heroic Soviet general of the war, Marshal Zhukov, would lead the festivities from his gallant white horse. Stalin stood on the sidelines and watched with envious eyes as this beloved war hero waved to adoring Russians who swelled with pride to see their brave general back home in Moscow. Yet while most Russians looked upon Zhukov with unbridled love and admiration, Stalin could only feel fear and hate.

For Stalin, someone who was this loved and respected could only mean one thing: a threat. Falling back on the brutal strategy that had kept his rivals at bay, and him in power for so long, Stalin prepared to rid himself of the beloved war hero. As 1945 drew to a close, Stalin began leveling accusations against General Zhukov, accusing him of plotting a coup.

Normally such accusations would mean immediate execution, but due to Zhukov's status as a national hero, Stalin managed to somewhat curtail his envy, wrath, and paranoia, and simply had Zhukov demoted and sent to a post in the Far East, as far away from him and Moscow as he could place him. In his postwar order Stalin didn't have room for any extra heroes; in typical Stalin fashion, he needed to take all of the glory for himself.

Conclusion

"Even now we feel that Stalin was devoted to Communism, he was a Marxist, this cannot and should not be denied."

—Nikita Khrushchev

By the time of the July 1945 Potsdam Conference, in which the two newly-christened superpowers of the United States and the Soviet Union dictated the terms of the post-war world, Stalin is at the zenith of his reign. Despite his unquestioned authority and power, Stalin is in constant fear of enemies, both real and imagined; he reverts back to his old suspicions, becoming reclusive and withdrawn.

His whole life, Stalin was fighting a perceived class of enemies. The Tsarists, the Trotskyites, and the Germans were all readily available adversaries for Stalin to project his ire toward. However, with the early 1950s not yielding an obvious opponent, Stalin felt the urge to dig a little bit deeper in order to find his foes. Stalin was on the verge of another great purge on March 5th, 1953, when he died while his plans were still on the drawing board. Stalin would then be denounced three years later by his successor, Nikita Khrushchev.

Today there is a renewed admiration of Stalin, however, and most Russians tend to view him favorably as the man who turned Russia into a superpower. Modern Russia faces many significant challenges and now as in the past, and despite the demons of the past, many long for a strong figure such as Joseph Stalin to lead them through the turbulence. Stalin died over 60 years ago, but his conflicted spirit still haunts the Russian people to this very day.

Printed in Great Britain
by Amazon